D1417457

13-42

THE ENGINEERING
OF RESTRAINT

The Nixon Administration and the Press

By FRED POWLEDGE

A Report of the
American Civil Liberties Union

PN
4738
.P6

Public Affairs Press, Washington, D. C.

Published by Public Affairs Press
419 New Jersey Ave., S.E., Washington, D. C. 20003
Copyright, 1971, by the American Civil Liberties Union
Printed in the United States of America
Library of Congress Catalog Card No. 71-183606

INTRODUCTION

Professor Thomas Emerson of the Yale Law School, the nation's leading First Amendment scholar, has written about the dynamics of limitations on freedom of speech. Emerson observes that:

". . . Limitations are seldom applied except in an atmosphere of public fear and hysteria. This may be deliberately aroused or may simply be the inevitable accompaniment of repression. Under such circumstances the doctrines and institutions for enforcing the limitations are subjected to intense pressures. Moreover, while some of the more hardy may be willing to defy the opposition and suffer the consequences, the more numerous are likely to be unwilling to run the risks. Similarly, persons whose cooperation is needed to permit the full flow of open discussion—those who own the means of publication or the facilities for communication—are likely to be frightened into withholding their patronage and assistance."

These conclusions were reached on the basis of Emerson's review of what he describes as "two outstanding eras of suppression in our past—the period of the Alien and Sedition Laws and the First World War."

Fred Powledge's report suggests that Emerson's conclusions would be equally warranted in assessing the present period. With the exception of the government's extraordinary efforts to restrain *The New York Times* and other papers from publishing the Pentagon Papers, the recent activities of the federal government may not have been quite as blatant and as heavy-handed as at the time of the Alien and Sedition Laws or during the First World

War. However, the press today is more vulnerable to subtler pressures. It is so vulnerable because it is more a business enterprise and, therefore, subject to economic pressures. And it is especially susceptible to pressures in that part of it—the broadcast industry—which is both the most significant in molding public opinion and which is directly subject to federal regulation.

ARYEH NEIER

PREFACE

This report is not a scientific survey. It does not claim to reflect a representative cross-section of American journalism within plus or minus five percentage points. It is, however, based on a large number of interviews and conversations with a variety of experts in the field, a great amount of reading, and several years of the writer's observations both as a working newspaperman and as an interested reader, listener, and viewer.

More than forty-five people contributed their opinions and recollections to the report. They range from a wire-service reporter, who says he has been radicalized by the events of the past few years, to the press secretary of Vice President Agnew, who blames the press for the nation's polarization, to the Washington bureau chief of the Underground Press Syndicate, who once threw a pie in the face of a member of the U.S. Commission on Obscenity and Pornography.

One section of the country is over-represented here. It is what Vice President Agnew has called "the geographical and intellectual confines of Washington, D. C., or New York City." And one broadcasting network—the Columbia Broadcasting System—is also examined more closely than its competitors. This paper makes no apology for these apparent biases: the bulk of the news, and of the news action, takes place in Washington and New York, and, theoretically, at least, the press is more widely represented, more competitive, and more inclined to be free there than elsewhere. If the press is having a hard time in the intellectual confines of Washington and New York, the theory went, then we are in trouble.

3

CBS is over-represented because it is the network which treats news and public affairs most seriously, and because it is the network that has come in for the most attack from government. Again, the theory went, if the best of commercial television is having trouble, then everybody is having trouble.

Anyone seriously interested in the future of the press in America (and in these perilous times, that should include very many of us) would do well to keep an eye on the growing body of internal criticism that is being produced by the press, particularly the written press. Such journals as the *Chicago Journalism Review* (a monthly published at 11 East Hubbard Street, Chicago, 60611, for $5 a year) and the *Columbia Journalism Review* (a quarterly published at the Graduate School of Journalism, Columbia University, New York City, 10027, for $6 a year) fill a long-standing need for criticism in a craft that once refused to admit it had any faults.

It may be noticed that some of the newsmen and executives whose thoughts are recorded in this report are quoted anonymously. Any newsman, experienced in asking people questions and trying to get their honest answers, will readily understand why the names are not attached. "Government sources," "a source close to the White House," "unimpeachable sources," (and, as Charles Pou used to occasionally put it in *The Atlanta Journal* when he was covering Georgia politics, "highly impeachable sources") are all people who want to answer your question but who also want to maintain a little job security. Newsmen, when talking about their craft, are not much different.

FRED POWLEDGE

THE ENGINEERING OF RESTRAINT

American governments have never gotten along harmoniously with the press. A wide-open government whose every important act is explained to the public has never been achieved and nobody seriously thinks it will be.

Rather, through the years the press and the government have developed an elaborate game. The side that is called the government—the elected officials, the appointed executives, the various bureaucracies and bureaucrats—puts out only the information it wants to put out. Through its vast network of public information offices, the government affirmatively broadcasts its side of the story, leaving out facts that might cloud the picture it wants to present. Through carefully-orchestrated leaks and "background" sessions with the press, individual officials are able to test the public on information and ideas for which they don't want to be held responsible. And through the device of simply not replying to questions it does not like, the government effectively prevents the public from getting other information. Over the years, officials of the governments, particularly the federal government, have become as adept at playing this game as they are at drawing up yearly budgets. They play with a cynicism that suggests a good measure of contempt for the public; but still they allow information to go out in quantities unequalled by other forms of government.

The more experienced and sophisticated representatives of the press—the reporters and editors, columnists and producers—play their side of the game with equal expertise. They accept the mimeographed press releases only at face value, treating them as the mere tips of icebergs. They report the leaks and the backgrounders with the skepticism they deserve. And they take the official "no comment" as the starting point, not the final word, in investigations that lead, often in classic detective-story style, from one seemingly unimportant fact to another.

The relationship has almost always been an adversary one, with each side working quite hard in the interests of its client (in this case, both sides claim to represent the same client), and, like adversary proceedings in the courts, frequently both sides have been able to cap off a day of passionate argument with a friendly drink at a nearby bar.

In recent years, though, that relationship has deteriorated. The federal government has sought to change the rules of the old game. Attacks on the press by the officers of government have become so widespread and all-pervasive that they constitute a massive federal-level attempt to subvert the letter and the spirit of the First Amendment.

The attempts have been dramatic—as in the case of the government's attempts to prevent publication of the Pentagon Papers by *The New York Times*. They have been repressive: as in the case of clumsy attempts to subpoena reporters, their notes, and newsfilm; and as in attempts, less clumsy and far more successful, by the intelligence establishment to pose as members of the press and thereby undermine public confidence in newsmen.

These assaults have not resulted in widespread criticism from the public, which will suffer the most if they are successful. Nor have they produced a concentrated, all-out reaction from the press itself, a reaction aimed at stopping the repression and preventing its recurrence. They have been bipartisan; the history of governmental interference with the press has spanned several recent national administrations. But they have been mounted with greater intensity and frequency during the present administration.

The chief actors in the current drama have been Vice President Spiro Agnew, through speeches and public comments which have incited a public (largely ignorant of how the press operates) against the bearer of seemingly worsening news; Attorney General John Mitchell, both in his capacity as chief prosecutor of the press in recent cases and as chief political advisor to the administration; President Richard Nixon, through his reluctance to put a stop to the assaults; and, the press itself, through its disinclination to raise further controversy by energetically resisting the government's attempts. The chief victims are the people of the United States, to whom the First Amendment belongs.

The most significant result of the attacks, so far, has not been a series of court and administrative rulings permanently restraining the freedom of the press; for, although the administration is attempting to obtain such restraints, it has, in one sense, so far failed. Rather, it has been the subtle tendency—almost impossible to document or measure—of the press itself to pull back; to consider the controversiality of its actions before it takes them, and then, in some cases, not to take those actions—to engage in self-censorship.

Executives from newspapers, television and radio, when asked during mid-1971 about current and developing patterns of government-media relations, almost invariably used the words, "chilling effect," to describe what they saw around them.

"Chilling effect" is a lawyer's term, a phrase from a court decision that, like "reasonable man" and "clear and present danger," has become a part of the legal vocabulary. The term comes from the 1965 Supreme Court decision in the case of *Dombrowski* v. *Pfister,* which grew out of the arrest of three civil rights proponents on charges of violating Louisiana's "antisubversive" act. Rather than merely fighting the state's charges, the three brought their own suit in federal court, seeking to enjoin the state from prosecuting. In what is considered a landmark decision, the U.S. Supreme Court upheld a lower federal court's injunction against the state, saying in part:

"A criminal prosecution under a statute regulating expression usually involves imponderables and contingencies that themselves may inhibit the full exercise of First Amendment freedoms . . . The chilling effect upon the exercise of the First Amendment rights may derive from the fact of the prosecution, unaffected by the prospects of its success or failure."

It is this sort of chill that representatives of the news craft

7

say has descended on reporters, editors, producers, and network executives in recent times. It started, they all agree, at the time of Vice President Agnew's November, 1969, Des Moines speech which simultaneously criticized the television networks and reminded them that they enjoyed "a monopoly sanctioned and licensed by government."

The chill came, these newsmen say, not out of an inability on the part of the press to take criticism (indeed, all of Agnew's criticisms had been voiced publicly before by thoughtful members of the press), but out of the quality of the criticism. In the Des Moines case, it was criticism which clearly reminded broadcasters of their licensed status. In Agnew's Montgomery speech, a week later, it was the "monopolization" enjoyed by certain newspapers.

And, adding to the chill, the criticism was combined with action—the most dramatic example being the Justice Department's recent attempts to impose censorship on *The Times* in the matter of the Pentagon Papers. Said one broadcaster, a man responsible for deciding what goes on and stays off a local station's Six O'clock News: "It's a matter of deciding that a project you want to undertake, and that you *would* have undertaken before, just might not be worth the trouble to undertake now. It's the worst form of censorship, I think. It literally chills me when I think about it and see it, and I *have* been seeing it."

The list of government actions, both subtle and dramatic, against the print and broadcast media has become a lengthy one since the fall of 1969. As of this writing—the beginning of the fall of 1971—attacks on the press have been mounted by all three branches of the federal government: from the executive, the Agnew speeches; from the legislative, an attempt to cite a television network for contempt, along with various pieces of proposed legislation clearly in conflict with the First Amendment; from the highest court in the land, a period (brief, but unprecedented in the nation's history) during which a newspaper was restrained from printing a news story. And, in the wake of the federal moves, lesser jurisdictions have made their own attempts at interfering with the press.

In a relatively short period of time, the press in the United

States has moved, and has been moved, from what many considered a position of extreme security to one of extreme vulnerability. There are some who say freedom of the press is now in the greatest degree of danger of being lost in America; there are others who say it is all but lost already.

*　　*　　*

Some newsmen see the current chill as a chicken-or-egg question: Did the Vice President, in his 1969 oratory, inflame a relatively neutral public into resentment against the press, or did he tap the handy reservoir of resentment that was there anyway? The evidence is on the side of the second explanation.

For many years, the press has been serving at home and abroad as the messenger who delivers the bad news, and all that was needed was a public figure such as Agnew to cultivate and organize the public around a movement to slay the messenger. This is what happened in the South in the Sixties, when the white citizens of a town in crisis could equate the arrival of the press with embarassing public revelations of the town's imperfection. Quite a few fair-minded reporters were despised in those days, and some were roughed up. One was killed. Now, as an entire nation's imperfections are being revealed, there is no section of the country or class of citizen which can expect to escape the spotlight.

Political figures have known all this for years. They knew, as did the vice president, that the press (both broadcast and printed media) is not the strong monolith that it might appear, but rather a delicate and vulnerable institution, and that a little bit of attack can go a long way, especially in times of civil chaos and national guilt over foreign affairs. Furthermore, Agnew's attacks coincided with the "discovery," first by the national administration and later by the press, of what has been called "middle America," a mythical concept that nevertheless rings many bells in many persons' heads, one of which is the idea that the press is somehow more to blame for the nation's troubles than are its citizens and elected leaders.

There is little scientific evidence to back up the above observations, but there is some: Hazel Erskine, the polls editor of

9

the *Public Opinion Quarterly* (and a member of the national board of directors of the American Civil Liberties Union), has analyzed various polls relating to the public's feelings about the press. Direct comparisons are impossible to make, she says, because survey questions that have been asked representative Americans at various times have not been worded similarly. But she has been able to conclude that "It does appear from the flimsy evidence available . . . that the barrage of criticism that the vice president has been broadcasting has at least coincided with a period when the American public has reached a low opinion of the news media."[1]

And there is the unscientific, but empirically-founded, evidence of newsmen themselves, many of whom see the public now as a good deal more resentful of their presence on the scene of a news event. Ned Schnurman, the city editor of WCBS-TV, New York, said: "It used to be that a reporter would get turned away from a meeting or something, and he'd bully his way in by saying 'The press has a right to know.' It isn't that way anymore. The word's getting around now that the press doesn't *have* to know any more."

At any rate, the Agnew speech of November 13, 1969, in which he criticized television, and one seven days later in which he took on East Coast newspapers, marked the beginning of a small era of verbal assault on the press.[2] To be sure, they were only words—words that Agnew referred to in one of his speeches as "the rough and tumble of public debate"—but considering where the words came from, and the references to licensing and monopolies, they had to be construed as warnings, as efforts at in-

---

[1] In the Winter, 1970-1971, issue of *Public Opinion Quarterly*, Ms. Erskine cited "some scattered bits of evidence" from polls that the vice president's attacks "have not been without effect on the U.S. public": A Harris poll early in 1970 showed that 56 per cent of the Americans surveyed thought Agnew was right in criticizing the way TV networks cover the news. A Gallup poll found a decline in the percentage of citizens who thought TV news was fair and impartial. And before the Agnew speeches 50 or 60 per cent thought the press "should have a free hand in its reporting of the news," while afterward a CBS News telephone poll reported "only 42 per cent of the U.S. public advocating freedom of the press."

[2] For details on the assault, and the reactions it provoked, along with details on other points raised in this paper, see the Appendix.

timidation, and as examples of government harassment of the press.

Vice President Agnew and others in the administration who spoke on the subject of the press were uniformly careful to add that they were not advocating censorship or actual governmental interference; but the threat was there and the repeated denials served only to call attention to it. As Dr. Frank Stanton, the president of CBS, said after the second Agnew speech: "It is far more shocking to me that the utterances of the second-ranking official of the United States government require such repeated assurances that he had in mind no violation of the Constitution than it is comforting to have them at all."

If the small era of verbal assault had stood by itself, it would not have attained much more significance than the oratory of a politician at election-time—deplorable, but at least understandable, plays on what the politician takes to be one of the public's fears. Unfortunately, the verbal assaults clearly had the backing of the Nixon administration; unfortunately, they were coordinated with action. Broadcasters and newspaper executives who believed Agnew's claims that he was not calling for censorship soon found that the federal government was on a path that would lead directly, by the summer of 1971, to nothing but censorship.

Chronologically the major events unfolded this way:

• Agnew, in his Des Moines speech, attacked television networks for their alleged "instant analysis and querulous criticism" of a speech President Nixon had made a few days before on Vietnam. But it was also revealed that Dean Burch, a Nixon appointee who only recently had been installed as head of the Federal Communications Commission, had asked networks for transcripts of their commentaries on the presidential speech—a rare departure from FCC protocol. A spokesman for Burch said his request was "basically one for more information." Others saw it as intimidation.

• At about the time Agnew was making his speeches, federal investigators were subpoenaing the files and unused photographs of *Time, Life,* and *Newsweek* as part of an investigation into the Weathermen.

• In January, 1970, federal prosecutors in San Francisco

11

issued subpoenas to the Columbia Broadcasting System, directing the network to hand over the film, used and unused, that it had collected while putting together a program on the Black Panthers and demanding a complete record of CBS's correspondence, internal notes, and telephone calls made in connection with the program. The network complied.

Then the government went after a big television name as well. Mike Wallace, the CBS correspondent who worked on the show, recalled that he was approached by a Justice Department press aide who asked him to testify in person. "He figured," said Wallace, "that because he knew me, I would come in and tell the attorney general what I knew about the Panthers. Conceivably that would be the first olive out of the bottle: If Wallace would do it, maybe some other people might do it." Wallace said the "threat of subpoena" hung over the discussion, but that he declined because he knew that "Once you get into that whole chain of being involved, it's like you're suddenly on a mailing list."

• The Justice Department was not so casual with Earl Caldwell, a black reporter for *The New York Times*. Caldwell had gained a considerable amount of trust among leaders and members of the Black Panther Party in the San Francisco area when, on February 2, 1970, federal prosecutors subpoenaed him for a grand jury appearance. One of the reported aims of the summons was to get evidence against David Hilliard, a Panther whom the government had charged with making a threat against the President's life in a speech.

Caldwell fought the demands on the grounds that his disappearance into the secret proceedings would wreck his relationships with dissident groups, who would never know what he did or did not reveal.

On June 5, 1970, Caldwell was held in contempt. He appealed to the U.S. Court of Appeals for the Ninth Circuit, which reversed the finding. The Justice Department then appealed to the U.S. Supreme Court, where the case is pending. (Further details of the Caldwell and other subpoena cases may be found in the Appendix.)

In the midst of the Caldwell controversy, the Justice Department issued a set of "Guidelines for Subpoenas to the News Media" which gave the impression that the department would be more careful in issuing future subpoenas. And Attorney General Mitchell announced plans to hold meetings with news executives in what one news story called "an unusual personal effort to ease the bitterness caused by a recent series of wide-ranging government subpoenas to newsmen."

The apparent drawback met with some skepticism. For one thing, the Justice Department was still trying to have Earl Caldwell found in contempt. Norman Isaacs, at that time a newspaper executive in Louisville and now on the faculty at the Columbia School of Journalism, expressed another view: "I'm of the old school which feels that you can almost never trust the government or politicians about what they're going to do next."

In the meantime, the government had demonstrated that it possessed an important weapon for chilling reporters who might want to do investigative work into complex social problems, and it had further demonstrated that it wanted to suppress what it thought of as the popularization of militant groups by the press. That the latter was in the government's mind is evident in its statement in the lower courts:

"Newsmen filing affidavits [in support of Caldwell] allege that they fear, in effect, that the Black Panthers will refrain from furnishing them with news. This contention is specious. Despite some assertions by Black Panther leaders to the contrary, the Black Panthers in fact depend on the mass media for their constant endeavor to maintain themselves in the public eye and thus gain adherents and continued support. They have continued unceasingly to exploit the facilities of the mass media for their own purposes."

Also in the meantime, as the Caldwell case took on more and more the characteristics of a landmark in the making, a court in California dismissed the threat charges against David Hilliard after the government refused to "disclose its logs of an electronic surveillance undertaken to protect itself from domestic subversion," as the U.S. solicitor general put it.

• A clear example of the sequential nature of government

attack was provided by a controversy over the lyrics of rock music. In September, 1970, Vice President Agnew, in a speech to Nevada Republicans, criticized the playing of songs on the radio that contained "drug culture propaganda." By the following March, the Federal Communications Commission had issued a notice to broadcasters holding them responsible for the airing of songs that would "promote or glorify the use of illegal drugs" and making it quite clear that a careless station might lose its license. (For details see the Appendix.)

• It was the legislative branch that moved against a broadcaster in the case of "The Selling of the Pentagon." CBS broadcast the documentary to about 9.6 million people, in 200 cities, on February 23, 1971. The show, which dealt with the awesome amount of money and effort the Penagon puts into projecting a favorable image of itself, was in many ways a standard documentary. Numerous television executives and newsmen, commenting on the ensuing controversy, remarked that any newspaper in the nation could have printed a story containing the same facts and caused not a ripple.

The television show, however, created a whirlpool. There was congressional outcry, particularly from Representative F. Edward Hebert, the chairman of the House Armed Services Committee. Vice President Agnew called the show "a subtle but vicious broadside against the nation's defense establishment." (For details of a related event see the Appendix.)

CBS rebroadcast the show a month later, and added 15 minutes of rebuttal from Hebert (who called it "un-American"), Agnew, and Defense Secretary Melvin Laird. Then, on April 8, 1971, Representative Harley O. Staggers, head of the House Committee on Interstate and Foreign Commerce (which concerns itself, among other things, with communications), issued a subpoena demanding all film used in the production, whether it went on the air or not. CBS President Stanton declined, saying, "The sole purpose of this subpoena is to obtain materials which will aid the committee in subjecting to legislative surveillance the news judgment of CBS in preparing 'The Selling of the Pentagon'."

By July the Staggers committee had voted to request from

Congress a contempt citation against CBS and Stanton. On July 13 the House voted 226 to 181 against issuing a citation. The vote was not necessarily a ringing reaffirmation of Congress's continuing belief in freedom of the press. For one thing, CBS mounted a strong lobbying effort to obtain a favorable vote for itself, and it is uncertain what would have happened had the defendant been less powerful. For another thing, the vote occurred not long after the courts' settlement of a censorship question in the Pentagon Papers case.

• Pressure from the executive branch resulted in a change of format in a network television show in the spring of 1971. As a controversy continued nationally over the nation's position on the supersonic transport plane, an assistant to Herb Klein, the President's director of communications, called the producer of the Dick Cavett Show, which is offered by the American Broadcasting Company, suggested that William Magruder, described by *Newsweek* as "the government's SST program manager," be a guest, and said that other recent guests on the show had been anti-SST.

The producer, John Gilroy, suggested a debate between Magruder and an anti-SST spokesman, but, according to *Newsweek*, the aide "insisted that Magruder go on alone." The White House won and Magruder appeared on the show. The news magazine reported that Gilroy had the feeling that the White House's request contained "a suggestion that ABC was in violation of the fairness doctrine."

• The most dramatic—and, in terms of the First Amendment, the most tragic—episode of government interference with freedom of the press came as a result of *The New York Times's* publication in June, 1971, of portions of a secret 47-volume government study of decision-making on Vietnam.

The government denied any interest in censorship,[3] but it

---

[3] The government was in court, said U.S. Attorney Whitney North Seymour in one of the earlier arguments, not to impose censorship but to promote law and order: "Contrary to some of the suggestions in (*The Times's*) argument . . . that what this amounts to is a bald attempt at suppression and censorship, we have attempted to approach the matter with the highest regard for the Constitutional rights of all concerned and in an orderly, lawful process." (For an assessment of the subsequent Supreme Court ruling in the case, see Melvin L. Wulf, "What's Fit to Print: Tragedy of 'The Times'," *Civil Liberties*, September, 1971.)

nevertheless tried to impose censorship on *The Times* and *The Washington Post* (which obtained the papers after *The Times*). It was the first time in the nation's history that such an attempt had been made, and it was successful. For 15 days, while the case shot up through the courts, *The Times* was restrained by court orders from continuing its publication of the material.

The U.S. Supreme Court ruled, 6-3, against suppression on June 30, but the decision did little to allay the fears of those who believed that the First Amendment meant Congress shall make no laws abridging freedom of the press.

*   *   *

By the end of the summer of 1971, less than two years after the Agnew speeches, the written and broadcast media had thus been shaken by a number of dramatic, severe (some would say permanently crippling) assaults on their freedom. And the public had sustained equally serious damage to its right of access to information.

But that was not all. There was much more evidence, less dramatic but certainly significant, that the government was embarked on a course that, if allowed to continue, threatens to erase the tradition of press freedom in this country and make public information subject to the whims of those in public office. The threat came not only from the federal government, but also from the lesser jurisdictions which seemed to be taking their cues from Washington.

By fall, 1971, there was a clearly-established pattern: some information was suppressed; other information was available only in the "official" version; those reporters who sought to go beyond the "official" version were frustrated, discredited, and, in some cases, punished for daring to cross the boundaries that government had erected.

Even as the controversy subsided over the publication of the Pentagon Papers, agents of the Federal Bureau of Investigation began questioning workers in the State Department in order to determine how information—"stories harmful to the national interest," in the words of a State Department spokesman—is leaked to the press. One instant result of the probe was to discourage

16

officials at State from talking with members of the press or returning their phone calls.

The intimidation was not reserved exclusively for the State Department. Officials at other government agencies have learned that, in the present administration, it is dangerous to talk to newsmen. Fred Graham, who covers Justice for the Washington Bureau of *The New York Times*, has found that his telephone calls to sources in two Justice Department divisions—civil rights and internal security—are routinely intercepted and re-routed back to the Justice Department public information office. "It's an example," he said, "of the chilling effect on the government itself." Graham explained that "when I'm calling someone in Justice who knows me and wants to talk to me, I have to give his secretary a phony name—a name that my source knows is me. When the secretary asks what my call is in reference to, I say 'personal'."

The issue of the press's access to government-held information became more significant in light of all the speeches, subpoenas, citations, and lawsuits. The press traditionally has fought for such information, and the government traditionally has tried to withhold it, but in recent times the government has strengthened its position with more and more massive efforts to blanket the press, and the public, with its own version of what's news.

In mid-1970 the Bureau of the Budget reported that federal agencies were spending $164 million on public relations. The sum did not include the White House public relations staff, which has been described as "the largest presidential-level PR staff in history."[4]

Late in 1970 President Nixon ordered a $48 million cut in what he called "self-serving" governmental public relations activities. But experienced, and therefore somewhat cynical, Washington reporters saw the move as an effort to centralize the control over agency PR as much as possible, and to centralize it in the hands of Herbert Klein, the first White House staffer in history to hold the title "Director of Communications."

Klein has not, in the opinion of many journalists, emerged as the "information czar" that some thought he would be. Sam

---

[4] Susan Wagner, "Publishing on the Potomac: The Selling of the Government," *Publishers Weekly*, August 8, 1971.

Archibald, the Washington director of the University of Missouri's Freedom of Information Center, pointed out in an interview that if a governmental publicist wanted to construct an information empire, he would probably start out with the title and powers of a Herb Klein. "But I don't think he's done that," said Archibald.

Another person familiar with the inner workings of the present administration (from his position inside the White House) pointed out that Klein's major contribution has been to convince high-ranking Nixon appointees, many of whom are distrustful of the press and unconvinced of its basic right to know anything, that they should nevertheless make themselves available to journalists.

Despite this unexpectedly good relationship with the Director of Communications, however, members of the press seem convinced that the government's management of information constitutes a prime obstacle to freedom of the press. As government and society have grown more complex, reporters have found themselves more and more at the mercy of the official spokesmen for governmental agencies for explanations of what's happening. W. Phillips Davison, visiting professor of sociology at the Columbia University School of Journalism, has pointed out that public relations sources in general originate between 40 and 60 per cent of the "news" that is to be found in the daily and weekly press of the United States. One of the government's most potent weapons, Professor Davison says, is withholding information.

There is ample evidence of the government's reliance on this weapon; it is found in abundance outside the boundaries of the United States, where U.S. correspondents must get the great bulk of their news from official government spokesmen in embassies, missions, and military installations. In Vietnam, the problem is compounded; the reporter's mere physical presence on the scene of a news event is contingent on the military's allowing him or her to be there.

Morley Safer, a CBS news correspondent, said in a televised discussion in March, 1971, that "in military situations, the only way to get there is with the military." Safer was reminded of the truth of his words a little later when he set out to do a story on Vietnamization. At the time, the controversy over CBS's "The

18

Selling of the Pentagon" was reaching its height. Everywhere Safer went in Vietnam, he was given the "deep freeze." Transportation was denied him and he returned without his story. The reason for Safer's troubles apparently was a memo from the U.S. Press Information Office in Saigon warning U.S. officials in the field that Safer was coming and noting that he had "ulterior motives."

Actual combat need not be in progress for a reporter to find himself dependent on the whims of public information officers. Louis Kraar, a Far East correspondent for Time-Life News Service based in Singapore, declared: "In most places, if you want to talk with someone in the U.S. embassy, you have to go to the press officer and he sets up the appointment. Even where this isn't necessary, the press officer tends to coordinate everything that goes out. One day in [one of the Southeast Asian countries], I was with the U.S. embassy press officer, talking, and he got a phone call from a diplomat. The diplomat said a reporter had approached him and asked for an appointment, and the diplomat wanted to know if the press officer recommended that he see the reporter. The press officer said 'Yes, but don't tell him anything'."

Transportation, said Kraar, is always a problem. "You propose a trip to an airbase in one of the Southeast Asian countries—say, Thailand. The U.S. says 'You can't visit them because the Thais don't want you.' You go to the Thais and they say 'We'd love to have you but the U.S. doesn't want you there.' Or the U.S. people will say 'We're not talking about this or that because we don't want to offend the host country.' Or 'That's classified.' You ask 'Why?' and they reply, 'Because it's sensitive.' And it turns out that they gave the same information to Congress a long time ago."

The military press itself has been subjected in recent years to numerous acts of harassment and censorship. How much more than usual it is difficult to determine, for previous wars were different from the current one in Indochina. Earlier wars were more popular among the young Americans sent to fight them; the youth culture, with its emphatic assertion of First Amendment rights, had not yet burst on the scene; and there was a great deal

19

of self-censorship among the editors of official military publications and broadcasting stations and among the operators of civilian-run newspapers for servicemen. Also, there was no underground military press in previous wars, and there is an active one now.[5]

χ It would appear that domestically, the government would have less control over the lives, writings, and travels of journalists. But the degree of control is enormous, and some newsmen maintain it is growing.

As Professor Davison has pointed out, much of what finds its way into print and onto the air as "news" originates at a public relations expert's typewriter. Experienced reporters traditionally have regarded press releases, or handouts, as only the starting point on a story, and experienced public information officials have learned not to be insulted when their mimeographed work is not taken at face value. They have accepted the fact that reporters will need more information, and they have become accustomed to arranging meetings and interviews with knowledgeable officials who can explain and analyze an event or a policy. These knowledgeable officials, by and large, have been middle- and higher-level career government employees, and their analysis usually has been accepted by reporters on a "background," or "not for attribution," basis and as material that is relatively devoid of partisan bias.

Often the information that is obtained from these officials is at odds with the interpretation that their superiors in the Cabinet or at the White House would like to see printed. Every recent administration has felt a degree of pain when such information has been published, but most have regarded the experience as

---

[5] When underground newspapers first appeared in the military in the late Sixties, along with coffeehouses and other unorthodox expressions of draftee discontent, the military engaged in blatant harassment of the offenders. It was not until 1969 that the Army was able to admit that dissent might be legal. A memorandum titled "Guidance on Dissent" was written; it noted, in part, that underground papers might not be published during duty hours or with Army property. "However," continued the memo, "the publication of 'underground newspapers' by soldiers off-post, and with their own money and equipment, is generally protected under the First Amendment's guarantees of freedom of the press. Unless such newspapers contain language, the utterance of which is punishable under federal law . . . authors of an 'underground newspaper' may not be disciplined for mere publication." (Quoted in Stephen G. Gross, "Military News Media Censorship," Freedom of Information Center Report No. 243, School of Journalism, University of Missouri at Columbia, June, 1970.)

one of the risks of operating in a democracy. The present administration, however, seems to have moved further than most in the direction of cutting off these sources of information.

As noted above, FBI agents have investigated recent leaks in the State Department, causing some officials to shy away from contacts with reporters. There are numerous other examples.

Murray Seeger, an economic specialist in the Washington bureau of *The Los Angeles Times*, noted in an interview that, for reporters in his field, two of the most important pieces of information are the periodic unemployment figures and the consumer price index. "For some years," said Seeger, "the Bureau of Labor Statistics decided that when it put the figures out, it would have on hand a group of experts to answer the reporters' questions." But in the spring of 1971, the briefings were cancelled by the Secretary of Labor. "This action followed a drop in the unemployment rate which the Secretary said was important," said Seeger. "He called it a turning point. But the analysts said it was statistically insignificant." The briefings were terminated, said Seeger, after economic reporters printed the analysts' version.

The stated reason for ending the briefings was that the statistics could be issued more quickly if analysts didn't have to spend time preparing charts and tables for the press. "The real reason," said a source in the government who felt he would lose his job if his name were used, "was that President Nixon has a genuine distrust of the career people in the Bureau of Labor Statistics. The trouble was that the White House, as always, underestimated the intelligence of the reporters. The reporters saw what was happening and they resented it."

Since the briefings ended, said the source, reporters have still managed to get all the technical information they need. "But they no longer can have the experience of asking very delicate questions of the experts in a group situation," he said, which adds an important—and sometimes embarrassing—dimension to the statistics.

In another case, reporter Seeger said, a government official had been designated as a contact for reporters covering the Council of Economic Advisors: "He used to give honest, off-the-record analyses of what was happening, but one of his comments appeared in the paper. He got a call from the White House saying either get on the team or off it." The spokesman responded by "not talking to the press at all," said the reporter.

Seeger, like many other journeyman reporters, insists that the obstacles only whet his appetite for information. "This administration historically does not trust the career, professional civil servants," he said. "They consider them all Democrats. And a good and experienced reporter can still get to those professionals and find out what's happening. This is very frustrating to the administration."

For reporters who are *not* so experienced, or those working under a deadline, or those who do not possess specialized knowledge of a field, a clever government information officer frequently can control what is printed by what he leaves *out* of a press release. But even when newsmen are able to assemble evidence of deception on the part of information officers, they often are reluctant to pursue the matter. Especially in the case of "beat" reporters, who cover a single field or agency on a continuing basis, there is a great urge to maintain "friendly" relations with the officials who, to a great degree, control the reporter's success or failure at getting the news.

Since the Fourth of July, 1967, the press has had at its disposal a law designed to liberalize access to government-held information. In practice, however, the Freedom of Information Act has been vastly underused by the media and vastly abused by the government. (For examples, see the Appendix.) It has been estimated that there are at least 20 million documents, including reproduced copies, that are currently "classified," and that less than 0.5 per cent of them "actually contain information qualifying even for the lowest defense classification."[6]

---

[6] From testimony of William G. Florence, retired "civilian security classification policy expert," at June, 1971, hearings of the Foreign Operations and Government Information Subcommittee of the House Government Operations Committee on "U.S. Government Information Policies and Practices." Florence, who worked at the Pentagon, further observed that "The majority of the people with whom I worked in the past few years reflected the belief that information is born classified."

Critiques of the act since its passage tend to agree that government agencies have continued to make it difficult for reporters and others to get information, either by mingling exempt and non-exempt material, by delaying action on requests, and in at least one case by requiring prospective viewers of such documents to give the nature of their interest and the purpose for which the material will be used—requirements which are clearly at odds with the act itself.

A number of reporters questioned recently about the usefulness of the Freedom of Information Act replied that it was almost nil. At best, they said, the act serves as a club with which they could threaten a bureaucrat who refused to provide information. And often, they said, a reporter who is in search of a piece of information will have more success getting it the old-fashioned way—that is, from government officials who prefer to remain anonymous—than through formal, and invariably lengthy, demands.

Sam Archibald, director of the Freedom of Information Center office in Washington (and a former staff administrator of the House Foreign Operations and Government Information Subcommittee), recently characterized the act as a compromise:

"So many exceptions were put into it that anybody can hold back information if he wants to. There are dozens of cases where an individual has gone to a government agency, asked for the information, been turned down, then *demanded* it, been turned down, pushed harder, and got it. There are dozens of other cases where reporters have phoned an agency, gotten turned down, didn't push, and didn't get it."

Walter Rugaber, an investigative reporter on the Washington staff of *The New York Times* who is known to his colleagues for his tenacity, has met with frequent denials of information from various government agencies, including the White House. "I asked for the guest list of a White House social function," said Rugaber, "and they wouldn't even give me that." Asked what he did then, the reporter replied: "In that case there was an easier way to find out, as is usually the case under Freedom of Information. It becomes a question of 'Who's going to look it up, me or them?' It becomes a reference problem."

Some problems are not so easily solved, though, as Rugaber and other reporters have discovered when they have attempted to get information on bids for government contracts. That door is almost always firmly closed, Freedom of Information Act or no Freedom of Information Act.

There are penalties for a reporter who digs too hard and makes himself too "obnoxious" in the eyes of government officials. Reporters know, for example, that the presidential press secretary will choose the members of the White House press corps who will serve as the "pool" reporters on presidential trips. Pool reporters stay close to the President and get better stories. Among the newspapers which have been in official disfavor is *The Los Angeles Times*. Before President Nixon's last State of the Union address, reporters were invited to background briefings on the address's various categories. *The Los Angeles Times* was not invited to any of them. "The standard punishment," said Murray Seeger of *The Times,* "is to cut off a reporter's channels of information as best they can. Some reporters fight back at this; some crawl around and try to be 'nice.' The degree of integrity of members of the press is about average, I'm afraid."

Sometimes the form of punishment is a good deal cruder. Jack Nelson, an investigative reporter for *The Los Angeles Times,* and one who has written articles critically analyzing the role of the Federal Bureau of Investigation, is presently considered "an enemy of the bureau," he says. Late in 1970 Nelson and Ronald Ostrow of *The Times* staff attempted to ask a number of questions of a high official of the FBI.

The official, Assistant Director Thomas Bishop, refused a verbal interview, answered some questions in writing, and refused to answer others on the grounds that they contained "strong overtones of harassment" and some were "so tainted with false and malicious implications that they frankly do not deserve the dignity of an acknowledgement." (For details on the exchange, see the Appendix.)

Nelson, meantime, has heard from colleagues that Bishop has referred to him as a man who drinks too much. William Eaton,

24

of the Washington bureau of *The Chicago Daily News,* has confirmed this. Eaton said he once asked Bishop for comment on Nelson's charges (in a book he co-authored, *The Orangeburg Massacre*) that the FBI had not done its job properly. "Bishop said something like 'You can't believe a guy who drinks a lot'," said Eaton. "He was commenting on Jack's drinking habits rather than answering my question. He made it clear that Nelson drank too much. He was trying to smear him. It had nothing to do with the merits of the case. It was a pure personal attack."

*　　*　　*

No matter how serious the differences between the government and the daily, "regular" press, no matter how many attempts are made by officials of the government to circumnavigate and defy the First Amendment, as long as the government is run by political people there will be at least a modicum of communication between the two institutions. Political people need the press in order to get elected, to promote their beliefs and policies, and to attack that which they do not believe in.

In recent years the need of politicians for the broadcast press has become greater—almost overwhelming. Simultaneously, the politicians have developed an extraordinary sensitivity about the broadcasters who report on their activities. Richard Salant, the president of CBS News, recalled in an interview not long ago a conversation he had had with John D. Erlichman, the assistant to President Nixon for domestic affairs. Erlichman had been a guest on a CBS morning show, and he and Salant had breakfast together afterward.

"In the middle of nice, small-talk conversation," said Salant, "he [Erlichman] suddenly lit into Dan Rather [CBS's White House correspondent] and called him a hatchet man and told me how unhappy they were with him.

"There were only two things I felt I ought to do, aside from telling him I thought Dan Rather was great. One was to make it public, and the other was to let Dan Rather know that he was now assured of being the White House correspondent as long as he ever wants to. But I can't guarantee that if the White House or somebody like Erlichman pulled the same stunt with some other broadcaster, the other broadcaster would react the way I did."

Neither, said Salant, could he guarantee that his reaction would insulate Rather from harassment by government officials: "He says from time to time he's getting the run-around and the deep freeze. But we have one thing going for us. We reach an awful lot of people, and a politician needs us. Even though he doesn't like us, he is still likely to want to be on our news broadcasts. So they don't boycott us. *Most* of them don't; Secretary Laird has boycotted us; he won't go on where he's subject to being edited. It's either verbatim or nothing, and I think we're going to get more and more of this. But the counterweight to that is most of them want to be on, most of the time."

There are, however, less orthodox elements of the press toward which the governments have adopted a policy of utter harassment. These are the underground press and its close relative, the campus press.

The underground press has grown tremendously in this country in recent years, and it has grown for many reasons—the need for channels of communication, other than rock music, to carry information from one youth community to another; the needs of young people with journalistic bents to fit their talents into the Woodstock Nation, and to do so nonviolently—with the written word—in the best American tradition. The most important reason, though, was that the "straight" press rarely attempted to explain what was happening in the youth culture, and that when it *did* attempt to explain, its explanations were aimed not at the youth themselves but at those who, because of their age or status, were outside the culture. And finally, the "straight" press seems in recent years to have lost its capacity or desire to engage in muckraking journalism, a form of communication which the underground press has been attempting, with infrequent success, to master.

From its inception the underground press has been harassed by representatives of the Establishment, often in the crudest of ways. All over the nation, vendors of underground newspapers have been arrested (sometimes on non-existent charges) and authorities have further attempted to suppress publications on the grounds of obscenity (often without even attempting to apply the Supreme Court's test). Harassment is directed at long-haired reporters from the underground press when they attempt to cover public news events (and even when they possess the "proper" police credentials, which sometimes are difficult to obtain). Photographers attempting to take pictures of plainclothes police agents, including FBI men, have been threatened. Filmmakers compiling documentaries about police repression have themselves been the victims of repression. (For details of typical cases of assaults on the underground press, see the Appendix.)

The offices of underground newspapers are believed by their inhabitants to be under continual surveillance. It is not difficult for an observer who possesses a healthy amount of paranoia to conclude that the authorities would treat the "straight" press in the same crude ways, if they thought they could get away with it. And increasingly—aided by vice presidential speeches, subpoenas from the Justice Department, "notices" from the FCC, citations from Congressmen, censorship by the courts; in short, what amounts to a widespread demonstration of the government's total contempt for the press and the First Amendment—the authorities are coming to the conclusion that they *can* get away with it.

As only one example out of many: When Vice President Agnew delivered a speech in Houston in May, 1970, half a year after his original attacks, *The New York Times* reported that "Numerous Secret Service Agents were in the area. One wore a press badge and two carried cameras and mingled with reporters. Agents later checked and rechecked some reporters' identification at the dinner."

The campus press, which serves communities where, according to tradition, fundamental democracy is taught, often is the victim of the most undemocratic actions. Suppression, censorship, and self-censorship are rampant in college newspaper offices. It could be argued that the campus press is a laboratory, not only for learning how to publish a newspaper under actual newspaper conditions, but also a laboratory for learning how to deal with an entrenched Establishment, largely politically motivated, that pays lip service to freedom but that seeks to use the press for its own

27

gratification and punishes the press when it resists. (Some examples of this may be found in the Appendix.)

*   *   *

Many of the attacks listed above are considered by the working press as little more than business as usual. It does not surprise a reporter to learn that a government official doesn't want the reporter to know something any more than it surprises him to learn that a press officer wants a press release to present a one-sided picture. To the reporter, there is little difference between the bureaucrats who say "No" now and those who said "No" during the previous administration. Indeed, many of them are the same bureaucrats. As Walter Rugaber put it, "I resent anybody's suggesting that it's any different under Nixon. Because it's the bureaucracy that does it. The day-to-day, grinding bureaucratic stuff is infinitely more invidious than the big, dramatic attacks."

But the day-to-day grind that is familiar to all newsmen has been accompanied by the big, dramatic attacks, and the sum of these is a chill.

The chill—the self-censorship—that is settling on the press in the United States is evident in all the media. It is evident least in the written press, but still it is there, and there it is growing.

Editors, perhaps fearing that they will be singled out for attack by a government official or agency, have started covering "middle America" more, which is laudable. But they also are covering ghetto America less. And in their quest for "balance" they too often seem to go overboard; to tell the story of the 5,692 murders that *didn't* happen today and somehow forget to tell about the one that did.

They adopt, without question, changes in the language dictated by the President. "Invasions" become "incursions"; "ghettoes" are no more, and the "Mafia" doesn't exist. But "hippies" and "self-styled revolutionaries" are still around.

They seem to have decided to live with the fact that the ranks of their reporters will be infiltrated by policemen. A few years ago, policemen openly posed as reporters at gatherings of "suspect" groups; the practice seems to have given way to one in which policemen no longer carry press credentials (issued by the police

28

themselves) identifying them as correspondents of fictitious newspapers and TV stations, but rather "hang around" on the fringes of the press conferences. Reporters tend to watch their language, and their questions, and their thoughts, in such situations. (See Appendix.)

In other newsgathering organizations, reporters think they have identified members of their own staffs who, they believe, serve as conduits to law enforcement agencies, notably the FBI.

Even the underground press, with its philosophy of commonplace repression, is not immune from the chill. Vendors of underground newspapers stop selling their product after they have been harassed a number of times by policemen. And, in the argument of a case involving *The Quicksilver Times* of Washington, D. C., there was testimony that the editors had planned to run a photograph but changed their minds because they knew it would bring on additional "hassling" of their street vendors. As the attorney for the newspaper argued, "It is almost impossible to imagine a more dramatic example of the kind of 'chilling effect' on First Amendment rights . . ."

Perhaps the most serious evidence of the chill on the print media could be found in *The New York Times's* handling of its case involving the Pentagon Papers. In its arguments before the Supreme Court against the government's move to restrain publication of the papers, *The Times* in effect proposed the abandonment of the First Amendment.

The government's argument had been that the courts may block the publication of secrets that involved a "grave and irrevocable" threat to the national security. *The Times's* lawyer, Professor Alexander M. Bickel of Yale Law School, said that if the president had an "inherent power" to enjoin the press from publishing, he should use it only in extraordinary circumstances. Bickel proposed the establishment of guidelines for prior restraint; such guidelines could be used only when publication of material would cause "direct, immediate and visible" harm to the nation.

Justice William O. Douglas then commented: "The First Amendment provides that Congress shall make no laws abridging the freedom of the press. Do you read that to mean that Congress can make some laws abridging freedom of the press?" It was, said Justice Douglas, "a very strange argument for *The Times* to be making."

* * *

In commercial television, the chill has become as ordinary as a station break. It is an accepted fact of life. This is the case for several reasons: For one thing, with the exception of the late Edward R. Murrow, television has little that could be called a tradition of fearless journalism. For another, television is extremely vulnerable because it is a governmentally-regulated industry. And television is *used* to being chilled; it is used to the chills of the rating game, the chills imposed on the networks by the affiliates, and of advertiser influence.[7] In fact, it frequently is difficult to tell whether an apparent network retreat (for example, CBS's movement of its "Sixty Minutes" show from a prime-time weeknight slot to the Sunday evening "intellectual ghetto") is the result of pressure from politicians or pressure from the almighty dollar.

Competent television newsmen are aware of this and it frustrates them. One of them, a well-known network correspondent, who said he had to remain anonymous, commented in an interview that network executives are "absolutely sincere when they talk about freedom of the press."

"But when they talk about licenses, are they really talking about freedom of the press, or freedom of a way to make money? I mean, when we're talking about our licenses, and attempts to put us out of business, and intimidation, what we're really talking about is a license to print money. These guys who manage the

---

[7] *Variety,* the show business weekly, provided an example of the continuing problem of advertiser pressure in April, 1971, when it reported that the agency representing Chesebrough-Ponds in its dealings with a new talk show, "Joyce and Barbara: For Adults Only," had "barred Ralph Nader from the roster of guest prospects." Experienced TV newsmen get incensed at what they call the myth that such pressure also extends to news and public affairs telecasts, but they overlook the fact that for millions of Americans, talk shows *are* a source of "news" and opinion on current events (as the Cavett-SST case illustrated). Advertisers still exert some influence on what gets left out of newspapers (the drunken-driving arrest of the heir to a department store fortune is likely to miss all editions of many American dailies, for example), but their power is not as specific as television advertisers, who contract to sponsor a single program, or part of one.

stations down the pike, who're so scared of the network: Do you think they really care about their news departments that desperately?

"*That's* the chilling effect. All along the line there are individual publishers—local affiliated stations—who are owned, some of them, by antediluvian, money-making, conservative-thinking entrepeneurs. And they'll see something that a network comes up with, like 'The Selling of the Pentagon' or a show on migrant workers, and it'll just curl their hair."

The correspondent said these station operators exert pressure, through their affiliate organizations, on the network itself.

"And that's where the chilling effect takes place. And the government knows an awful lot of these people. The administration knows an awful lot of them socially—it's nice to have some attention paid to you by the White House—and they let something drop, and so it becomes that kind of a chilling effect. So Spiro Agnew starts out with something, and he gets the kind of playback he wants, and it becomes a vicious circle, and he says, 'Gee, I have a constituency here.' And that constituency feeds on Spiro. And then the public begins to hear it. And it does have a snowballing effect, and we are in the middle of it and we're going to be hurt by it, eventually."

It has been argued that commercial television has already been hurt by the chill—hurt so badly that it is engaged in a full-scale retreat. Nicholas Johnson, the outspoken Federal Communications Commission member, said in April, 1971: "The Agnew-induced cowardice in the networks has produced some of the 'chilling effect' on free expression that the administration was out to encourage—and that the Supreme Court has used as a standard for governmental actions violative of the First Amendment. The mortality rate for network documentaries seemed unusually high after Des Moines."

Only a few days after Agnew's Des Moines speech, said Johnson, "the networks provided only spotty coverage of by far the largest march on the White House in American history. Upward of 500,000 angry Americans flooded Washington to protest the Indochina war; everyone was there, it seemed, except the

President and the network newsmen. David Brinkley—among others in network media—later acknowledged that this was an unfortunate decision.

"Contrast this with the lavish coverage of Bob Hope's 'Honor America Day' eight months later. There was no protest then from the Vice President; the President was obviously pleased to have the networks busy themselves with the apple pie view of America. Picking up the spirit of the times, ABC Sports banned halftime coverage of the Buffalo-Holy Cross football game because it had to do with the 'controversial' subject of peace but provided a nationwide audience for the chairman of the Joint Chiefs of Staff to say a few words on behalf of war at the halftime of the Army-Navy game."[8]

It might be expected that the chill would be less felt in the newsrooms of the networks' flagship stations, but newsmen there say it is worse, simply because the flagships are tremendous moneymakers for the networks.

John Wicklein, a journalist who recently departed from the newsroom of WCBS-TV in New York (he had been hired to bring a "new form of investigative reporting" into the station, then let go), put it this way:

"There was a tremendous fear of what the administration could do to that broadcasting station in terms of harassing it. The executives stated quite clearly that they felt CBS was the number one target of the administration. They really got their lawyers into everything. They said, in effect, to newsmen: 'Don't do anything that could get us a complaint.' People in the newsroom were just scared silly of controversy. They thought the network would like very much to get out of the area of controversy and into nothing but entertainment. In fact, there are some people there who think the network would like to get out of news altogether. I think the hard news has been destroyed there."

Wicklein recalled a story that WCBS-TV had done on an abortion clinic in New York City. Complaints followed the airing of the program, which included film of an actual abortion. Some

---

[8] Statement by Nicholas Johnson, April 1, 1971, quoted by Leon Friedman in manuscript in press.

of those who complained suggested that the abortion had been "staged." A network executive, said Wicklein, sent company lawyers to investigate. "They kept us on the grill for six weeks, cross-examining everybody involved to see if they could find discrepancies in our stories. It shook the whole news staff. They got the message. The message was, 'Don't do controversy'."

A newsman still employed at WCBS-TV confirmed what Wicklein had said, and added:

"It becomes a matter of deciding *not to do things*. The network which owns us is aware of its difficulties with the feds in the past, and they're unwilling to trust their own news judgment to do something that might be 'controversial'."

He cited the case of a former government expert in Southeast Asia, knowledgeable about the Laotion refugee situation and critical of U.S. efforts there, who was available for a television interview. The station did the interview, but it never made the air. The newsman said:

"We pass up things like this, and we make various excuses for it, but what it boils down to is bending over backward to avoid criticism. These are non-conscious, non-verbal decisions by executives to do or not do something.

"The attempts to curb television have been clumsy and public so far. So the publishers and broadcasters have gotten their backs up. But: Everytime something comes up, they retreat a little."

Another broadcaster who is concerned about gradual retreat is Richard Salant, the CBS news president. Salant is one of the handful of television executives today who appear to be trying to establish a proper tradition of television journalism. Perhaps for that reason, Salant's news operation at CBS has come in for the most concentrated attack from agencies of government. Some of the politicians, said Salant, are "doing it to bully us."

"And they know that they can scare the pants off almost any broadcaster—certainly the affiliates. It takes an awful lot of guts for management to ignore these attacks, because they can literally mean their economic life.

"We get a letter (from the FCC, notifying the network of a complaint from the public), and everybody has to dig. The reporters who produced the show, everybody has to dig out stuff and try to reconstruct why they did what they did, and it has literally a chilling effect. If nothing else, it takes you away from your work. And when the government, through the FCC, moves into these areas, it's *chilling*. We have more lawyers than we have reporters."

Salant said the Federal Communications Commission, in recent years, had shown more sympathy for the effect of such complaints on the networks, and that the FCC was "coming to a realization that there ought to be a high threshold before they automatically send these letters on to us." But the chill had come more recently from other areas, he added:

"You remember in that first speech, Agnew went after us, and in the second one he broadened it to go after *The Times* and *Post-Newsweek*. Six weeks after that second speech a group of people, all of them former business associates or friends of Nixon's, joined together to apply for the license in Miami of the station owned by *The Post* and *Newsweek*. Ultimately that was dropped.

"Whether it was coincidence or not, the important thing about this was the shock wave this caused among the stations around the country who read it to mean that if they didn't make the networks behave themselves, and if they didn't appeal more to middle America, they were going to be faced with this kind of thing. And a license contest is a very difficult and very expensive thing. It's capital punishment. So these guys decided to play it safe.

"After Agnew, we had much more concerted criticism from the affiliates. I've always been convinced—although Herb Klein denies it—that there has been a deliberate effort on the part of the administration to exploit the natural abrasions between the affiliates in the first place. Their notion of news, you know, is different from our notion of news.

"They're part of the local establishment. The news, to them, is saying what the mayor said, and so on. And we have distinct signs of the administration's wooing the stations and encouraging them to stand up and fight us."

As an example of his last statement, Salant offered the case of a move about a year ago by members of CBS's affiliate advisory board to send a delegation to New York to tell CBS management "how unhappy they were with our Vietnam coverage" and then to send the delegation on to Saigon to let CBS reporters in the field know too. Said Salant:

"It was an atrocious idea, and we finally persuaded them not to do it. The fellow who was presenting this idea finally told somebody that it wasn't his idea; that it was an idea that was proposed by another affiliate to him after he'd been to a meeting at the White House. Somebody—we don't know who—at the White House had said, 'Aren't you unhappy with the way they're covering Vietnam?' He said 'Yes, I am.'

" 'Well, why don't you do something about it? Why don't you go out to Saigon and tell them so?' "

The CBS executive said that he did not think the reported attempt by the White House was naive.

"No, sir. I think it's very clever. We have two very soft underbellies. One is the affiliates, who have the perfect right under the law, and the obligation, to turn down everything from the network that they don't want. They can put us in news completely out of business by simply turning off the faucet. Our second soft underbelly is our licensing. There's no solution to either problem."

Salant fears that if things progress in the direction they seem to be headed, one result will be the fragmentation of the press, with each publication and station "carving out for itself that segment of the political audience it wants to appeal to, and giving them what they want, so there's never really any cross-fertilization."

He said he feared a rival network, ABC, had "already decided to go after middle America" with its "Happy News" (a feature of ABC's New York flagship station which currently is at the top of New York's viewer ratings) and, Salant said, with attempts by ABC President Leonard Goldenson to woo major advertisers with the argument, Why should you spend your money on CBS, which is always in trouble with the administration? Salant said "a number of sales executives" had told him about the latter.

James C. Hagerty, the vice president for corporate affairs for the American Broadcasting Companies, Inc., said he had "no knowledge" of Goldenson's making such a pitch. Hagerty also said the record would show that ABC was not making any special appeal to any segment of the population, and he pointed out that the producers of WABC-TV's "Happy News" hour are just "people who don't think they have to be prophets of doom all the time."

Salant's overriding fear, he said, is of self-censorship:

"I have a constant fear that somebody down the line—reporters, or producers, or somebody—will think, 'Gee, we've caused such headaches to management, or to ourselves, in having to dig out all this stuff when the lawyers come around: I'll play it easy for a while.'

"Well, the first thing I did after the Agnew speech was send out a memorandum saying it's a high crime if this happens. But one always has to worry about this. I haven't seen any signs of it yet. But it's a very frightening thing. You have to be as noisy as possible to guard against it.

"I think this is something that's increasing. I think it's going to get worse and worse and worse and worse and worse. I don't think we've seen the climax of it, and I don't think it's passing. The tendency is to say 'Oh, well, this isn't the ideal one to fight, so let's let this one go'."

* * *

Those who run commercial television, with some notable exceptions, have become accustomed to working in a chilly atmosphere. They have devised ways of accommodating themselves to their environment, and that is an infinitely more tragic state of affairs than a speech made by a vice president or a contempt citation sought by a congressman. For public television, which only now is beginning to achieve some sort of national structure of its own, an entirely new set of chills is present.

The danger most often cited by critics of public television—and by some of public television's own executives—is the source of its funding. Public TV, through the Corporation for Public Broadcasting, which was created by Congress in the Public Broadcasting Act of 1967, currently is receiving $35 million from

Congress, and thus is intimately dependent upon the whims of government and of political people for its very existence.

The quality of the criticism from those who believe that public television has already knuckled under is notable for its intensity. The critics (many of whom are present or former producers of documentary shows for the New York-based National Educational Television which used to be the public TV network) speak of directives from Washington, public TV's new headquarters, banning "controversial" material and avoiding blame for shows that outrage some elements of society. They say, too, that national public television's 1971-72 schedule will be almost devoid of hard-hitting, tough documentaries. Said one newsman, now a commercial TV executive and formerly a NET documentary producer:

"Public television is so immersed in its problems about congressional funding that it's impossible to measure the degree to which they're caving in to pressure. But it's enormous. I left public television because they wanted to send me to Washington, and there was the clear understanding that they wanted me to do pretty much what the government wanted. They tend to be concerned with programs that will be of interest to Congress, so that members of Congress can literally *see* your cameras at a hearing and know that the money they were appropriating was being used 'wisely'."

Said another former public television employee who also wished to remain anonymous:

"Public television is, if anything, even more craven than commercial TV now. There is direct censorship: word coming from Washington to the production center, directly, saying 'You can't do this; it'll jeopardize our appropriation.' The producers are told not to come up with any controversial ideas; it'll 'get us into trouble.' The era of strong documentaries is dead. The people in Washington are saying 'Later on we'll get independence; don't rock the boat now'."

Alan Levin, a producer of documentaries at WNET-TV, Channel 13, New York City, and formerly a producer for NET (where he did "Who Invited Us?", an investigation of U.S. involvement in developing nations), feels that the re-organization of public television around the Corporation and the Public Broadcasting Service will result in the production of non-controversial programming for most of the nation's 205 public TV stations. This, he thinks, is because most of those stations are afraid of controversy.

But stations serving "unusual" communities will be allowed to indulge in controversy, he said. "They want one relatively serious operation at Channel 13," he said, "because if they didn't have that, they'd have to fold up their little experiment in democracy and go home. Their feeling is, 'Let the freaks have one station.' But even that isn't true; 13's padded with a lot of pap."

Bill Greeley, who covers public television for *Variety* and who probably is privy to more of the industry's information than any other reporter, feels that the medium is definitely "shying away from controversial shows"—so much so, he says, that a program like "The Selling of the Pentagon" could not now be shown on public TV. Of the work of the Corporation, he says: "All the projects they're into are pleasing to the government, and especially pleasing to the Nixon administration."

┼Public TV's fall, 1971, schedule, said Greeley, demonstrated the degree to which the chill has taken over: "This year the hard-hitting documentaries and the muckraking are all gone. They've got a Monday night 90-minute slot for opera, drama, and some documentaries. They're clearly shying away from controversy."

Executives of public television deny these criticisms. There will be as many hard-hitting documentaries as there were last year, they say. But they do not deny that they are aware of their relationships with Congress. Other problems are more important, though, they say; one of the most important being the internal criticism that permeates public TV.

William E. Duke, public affairs director for the Corporation for Public Broadcasting, said in an interview that in two and one-half years he had "received four or maybe five indications of any kind from Capitol Hill on any kind of programming. Most of them were questions of matters of fact, and a couple of them were right. Congress is not so much a problem as the individual stations."

For years, Duke said, public TV stations around the country had to take what they got from NET in New York or get along on nothing. NET's output was "material that they considered elitist; stuff that would be applauded at a New York cocktail party." Now, he said, public television promises to do a better job of serving the entire nation.

Duke does not expect the New York producers or Bill Greeley to enjoy this: "Sometimes I think there's a death wish in public television, a feeling that we shouldn't succeed. It's like the reform Democrats in New York City. We've gotten as far as we have on baling wire and 'Sesame Street' and it looks as if it's possible that we may come up with something that may last. And then some of the critics come along and say 'Somebody must have sold out because that's not possible'."

Hartford E. Gunn, Jr., is the president of the Public Broadcasting Service, the programming and scheduling arm of national public television. Like the Corporation, PBS is physically situated in Washington and is regarded with intense skepticism by the New York producers.

"I have political problems," said Gunn in a recent interview. "But they're *internal* political problems." He gestured in the direction of New York City. Of Congress he said:

"If you see a long-term benefit to what you're doing, I think you make certain calculations. You can argue that these have a chilling effect or that they don't have a chilling effect. But everybody makes calculations. You would think me stupid, and I would indeed *be* stupid, if I or anybody in this system said we were not aware of the context in which we're working; that we're not aware that there are certain limitations. So the question, as I see it, becomes, 'Are those limitations crippling?'

"We haven't walked away from any topic. We have never said that the treatment should be superficial . . . And I'm prepared to defend that, to open the files to anybody who wants to make a serious investigation of what's been submitted to us and what we've approved.

"Now, I don't know what goes on within the individual production organizations. I don't know the extent to which a producer might *feel* that we might not like something, and not offer it. I don't want that to happen. What I don't like about what's going on in the system at the moment is that, in a strange way, all the hue and cry is providing the chill."

Gunn said PBS was more concerned lest it appear to Congress as gutless. When the 1967 public TV act was being debated in Congress, Gunn was a station manager in Massachusetts, and he lobbied for the bill:

"And, strangely enough, the same concern on both ends of the spectrum, extreme right and the left of center, was precisely the same argument: That public TV will be a domestic USIA, a propaganda instrument. So in a strange way, no matter how we might feel that we've got to 'please' Congress—and I don't think that operates as a factor—the one thing that's likely to unite the left and the right would be that we were a propaganda industry. So those of us who sit here are especially sensitive to that. We do not want to get tagged with that."

*   *   *

In the final analysis, the magnitude of the chill is difficult, even impossible, to measure accurately. It is possible only to say it is there and to point it out when it is obvious: when a newspaper or television station does not cover a story that ordinarily would have been covered; or to wonder if a story that *has* been covered has been "toned down" somewhere along the line, and if so, whether the result is a story that is closer to the truth or more distant from it.

It is not so easy to measure other chills: A wire service reporter who thinks one of his editors is a conduit to the FBI says he warns his black militant sources not to tell him anything they wouldn't tell the police. A television producer says he has a colleague who decided not to invite a rejection, and so he didn't suggest a project that might be termed "too controversial." A black newswoman for a radio station says she wants to do a story explaining what people in the ghetto are really thinking, but she knows that "the management wouldn't sit still for that."

A newspaperman might want to do a story on marijuana use among his town's youth; he knows that in order to do a proper

40

job of research he must interview young marijuana users. But there is a chance (and, if the government prosecutors are successful in the Caldwell case, a likelihood) that he will be subpoenaed to testify in secret to a grand jury. Does the reporter decide not to do the story?

The decision *not to do the story* appears to be multiplying, all over the nation, and before long there will just not be very much interpretation of complex events and social movements. What will be left will be the relatively safe "hard" news of speeches and statements, and that can be easily manipulated.[9]

It is in these ways that the First Amendment is being lost, a little each day. It could, and should, be argued that the threat would not be nearly so great if the press itself had fought harder for its own freedom. But it must not matter that the press has chosen to approach this delicate matter with kid gloves on; the First Amendment does not belong to the press, but to the people, and they must not allow it to be given away or traded for a little respectability, or a little immunity from a politician's criticism.

---

[9] As witness the State of New York's manipulation of news about who killed hostages in the September, 1971, Attica prison uprising. A clearer example of governmental deception would be difficult to find, and yet many of those involved in the tragedy ended up despising the press for trying to tell them what had happened.

41

APPENDIX

The Agnew Attacks

The chain of events surrounding the Agnew attacks went like this: On September 26, 1969, Frank Shakespeare, Jr., the director of the U.S. Information Agency, fired the first volley in a speech at the annual convention of the Radio and Television News Directors' Association. Shakespeare, who maintained that he was speaking as a "private citizen" (a clear impossibility), said, "It is my view that TV news, as it exists in the country today, is rather clearly liberally oriented." He suggested that broadcasters take a prospective employee's ideology into consideration, and that they attempt to balance the liberalism.

On November 3, President Nixon made a speech on Vietnam. Network commentators, who had been provided with copies of the speech some time before, analyzed the remarks and generally found them a restatement of U.S. policy. Two days later, Dean Burch, who had taken office as head of the FCC six days before, asked the networks for transcripts of their commentaries.

On November 13, Agnew made his Des Moines speech criticizing television. The speech provoked instantaneous controversy. One day later, Director of Communications Herbert Klein said he agreed with Agnew's remarks, and he said the criticism should be extended to newspapers as well. "If you look at the problems you have today and you fail to continue to examine them," he said, "you do invite the government to come in. I would not like to see that happen." On the same day, White House press secretary Ronald L. Ziegler said, "There is absolutely no intention on the part of Herb or the Vice President to suggest that there should be censorship or there should be government intervention in this."

On November 19, Klein acknowledged that the White House had on occasion called television stations to ask what their editorial treatment of the President would be. On November 20, Agnew made his Montgomery speech on newspapers.

The Vice President has been relatively silent in recent months on the subject of the press, and an effort to gain an interview with him on the subject met with a refusal from his press secretary, Victor Gold. The press secretary granted his *own* interview, however, in which he said that the media frequently ask to see Agnew because they know what he says will build their circulation or listenership.

Gold, who at times raised his voice to a shout and pounded his desk in the Executive Office Building, maintained that the networks, especially, glory in what he called "commercializing the bad news," and that they thus have incurred the disbelief and wrath of the American public. The 11 o'clock news is bad enough, said Gold; "now there's no relief at 11:30 either. We used to have Steve Allen and Johnny Carson and *entertainment*, but now you get Gloria Steinem and Jimmy Breslin and Al Capp. Millions of Americans go to bed every night hating what they've just heard.

"I think the incessant and insatiable demand for controversy and conflict to *sell news* is the single most polarizing factor in American life today," Gold said.

THE CALDWELL CASE

It is unlikely that a subpoena from the government to a newsman will bring in much more information on a suspect individual or group than the government already has been able to compile, what with its widespread use of undercover agents, informants, and surveillance devices. More likely, the subpoena is an instrument used to fish for random incriminating information; to harass the reporter who learns too much; to cut down on the amount of "publicity" a dissident group gets; and, to serve notice on the press that the government does not consider it its equal, but rather its enemy. The last feeling is similar to the one exhibited by police against their underworld informants: The authorities hold an informant in great contempt, but they keep him around as long as he serves a useful purpose.

Reporters have testified, under subpoena and otherwise, for decades, but the Caldwell case is part of a relatively new pattern: The government is seeking information from reporters about political beliefs and life styles. Two other similar cases are to be argued before the U.S. Supreme Court in its fall, 1971 session. Paul M. Branzburg, an investigative reporter for *The Louisville Courier-Journal*, published stories in 1969 and 1971 on the use, manufacture, and sale of marijuana and hashish. Much of the story was based on Branzburg's personal observations of drug users, who admitted him into their confidence after he promised not to identify them.

Two separate grand juries summoned Branzburg to testify about what he had seen, and they demanded that he name names. Branzburg declined, citing the First and Fourteenth Amendments and a Kentucky statute which gives reporters immunity from disclosing "sources of information." The Kentucky Court of Appeals ruled that Branzburg's immunity did not cover what he personally observed.

In the case of Paul Pappas, a New Bedford, Massachusetts, television newsman, the reporter was allowed into a Black Panther headquarters during a period of civil disorder in July, 1970. The condition was that Pappas report nothing he saw or heard unless there was a police raid— which the Panthers expected. There was no raid, and Pappas reported nothing. He later refused to tell a grand jury what had gone on inside the headquarters. The state's highest court ruled that Pappas should talk, and that matter is now before the Supreme Court, too.

The Caldwell case is on appeal from the U.S. Court of Appeals for the Ninth Circuit, which rendered a decision in the reporter's favor on November 16, 1970. The decision said in part: "If the grand jury may require appellant to make available to it information obtained by him in his capacity as a news gatherer, then the grand jury and the Department of Justice have the power to appropriate appellant's investigative efforts to their own behalf—to convert him after the fact into an investigative agent of the government.

"The very concept of a free press requires that the news media be accorded a measure of autonomy; that they should be free to pursue their own investigations to their own ends without fear of governmental interference, and that they should be able to protect their investigative processes.

"To convert news gatherers into Department of Justice investigators is to invade the autonomy of the press by imposing a governmental function upon them. To do so where the result is to diminish their future capacity as news gatherers is destructive of their public function. To accomplish this where it has not been shown to be essential to the grand jury inquiry simply cannot be justified in the public interest. Further, it is not unreasonable to expect journalists everywhere to temper their reporting so as to reduce the probability that they will be required to submit to interrogation."

In September, 1971, as briefs were being submitted to the Supreme Court in the Caldwell case, the CBS and NBC television networks disclosed that between January, 1969, and July, 1971, they had received 122 subpoenas for film or reporters to testify in court or grand jury proceedings. Fifty-two of the subpoenas came from governments, the remainder from individuals.

DRUG LYRICS

In the case of radio stations playing modern music with lyrics referring to drugs, it became quite clear that Vice President Agnew's speeches had an enforcement arm. The sequence of events:

On September 14, 1970, the Vice President delivered a speech in Las Vegas in which he said, in part: "We should listen more carefully to popular music, because at its best it is worthy of more serious application, and at its worst it is blatant drug culture propaganda. . . . I may be accused of advocating 'song censorship' for pointing this out, but have you really heard the words of some of these songs?" Then Agnew went into a medley of Beatles and Jefferson Airplane lyrics.

He said his audience could help the situation by opening their eyes and ears to "the drug culture's message"; by being firmer with their families; and by electing Republicans.

On March 5, 1971, the Federal Communications Commission issued a public notice about drug lyrics. The FCC said it had received "a number of complaints" about "the use of language" in records played on the air "tending to promote or glorify the use of illegal drugs such as marijuana, LSD, 'speed,' etc." Broadcast licensees, said the Commission, must henceforth make a judgment "whether a particular record depicts the dangers of drug abuse or, to the contrary, promotes such illegal drug use." And "someone in a responsible position" at the station must know the content of the lyrics.

Not knowing what is being broadcast, said the FCC, "is clearly a violation of the basic principle of the licensee's responsibility for, and duty to exercise adequate control over, the broadcast material presented over his station. It raises serious questions as to whether continued operation of the station is in the public interest . . ."

There was considerable confusion over the notice (The Washington Evening Star headlined the story "Stations Told To Halt Drug-Oriented Music"), and on April 16, 1971, the FCC issued another statement that was said to clarify the situation, but that also attempted to soften the Commission's threat to jerk licenses. ". . . at renewal time," said the notice, "our function is solely limited to a review of whether a licensee's programming efforts, on an overall basis, have been in the public interest."

On August 4, 1971, the Commission, in response to a petition from broadcasters charging that there were inconsistencies in the rulings, said its April 16 opinion "stands as our definitive statement in this area."

Commissioner Nicholas Johnson, in a series of dissents to the FCC actions, called the first notice "an unsuccessfully-disguised attempt by the Federal Communications Commission to censor song lyrics that the majority disapproves of; it is an attempt by a group of establishmentarians to determine what youth can say and hear; it is an unconstitutional action by a federal agency aimed clearly at controlling the content of speech."

In a dissent on the Commission's August announcement, Johnson said: "Broadcasters—courageous and cowardly alike—are a pretty skittish lot. The administration, and the FCC, know that. Having been told—very loudly and clearly—that powerful people in Washington are interested in their records' song lyrics, all too many will go out of their way to select lyrics designed to please. At that point the government has succeeded in its purpose; it is then safe to issue all the apologies and rescinding statements necessary to silence the critics."

In the controversy over CBS's airing of "The Selling of the Pentagon," the Pentagon itself kept relatively quiet while its friends in Congress and the executive branch complained. The military was keeping an eye on things, however.

On the night of March 17, 1971, non-commercial television channel 31 in New York, WNYC-TV, broadcast a program in its series titled "All About TV," whose host, Steven H. Scheuer, is proud of the fact that his is the only program on television that seriously examines the medium. This particular program was devoted to an examination of the Pentagon flap, and CBS producers and a reporter were the guests.

There was a reference, part-way through the program, to a "General Harkin" who once said U.S. troops would be home from Vietnam by the Christmas of 1964. The following morning, according to Bernard R. Buck, WYNC-TV's program manager, the station's director received a telephone call from the Pentagon. It was from the office of Daniel Z. Henkin, the assistant secretary of defense for public affairs. Henkin, said Buck, objected to what he thought was an erroneous reference to himself as a general.

The only conclusion one could make, said Buck, was that the Defense Department had in some way monitored the program. "It's common knowledge that the department has people monitoring TV all over the country," he said. (Evidence of monitoring in the Washington area was revealed in June, 1971, when it was discovered that the Pentagon was advertising for small businesses to make verbatim records of "all newscasts emanating from all metropolitan area radio and TV stations." In 1970, the Pentagon had paid $20,000 for such work. Senator William Proxmire, learning of the advertisement, protested to Defense Secretary Melvin Laird. An aide to Proxmire said the Pentagon had replied that it just wanted to know what was going on and that the contracts were also good for small business.)

Asked if the WNYC-TV incident had had a chilling effect on his station, Buck said no. "It chilled *us* on the whole defense establishment," he added. "Before this came up, we used to run military-produced films and spots—'This is your army' sorts of things—but we don't any more. The feeling is why the hell should we be a party to this kind of thing?"

FREEDOM OF INFORMATION

Before the passage of the Freedom of Information Act, government agencies withheld information for a variety of reasons: They cited their general "housekeeping" responsibilities; department heads at the lowest level claimed "executive privilege"; even the Administrative Procedure Act of 1946, which was supposed to have made information more available, was used to suppress it.

There were numerous examples of serious absurdity. The Board of Engineers for Rivers and Harbors, which ruled on billions of dollars worth of federal construction projects, would not report its votes on "controversial" issues. Bureaucrats grew tired of "Top Secret" and "Confidential" and invented a classification named "Limitation on Availability Files for Public Reference." President Kennedy gave "Top Secret" power to the Peace Corps. The Department of Agriculture would not release results on a turkey marketing order in upstate New York. The Pentagon telephone directory, which was for sale to the public during World War II, afterward was classified "For Official Use Only."

All this was supposed to change with the passage of the act. President Johnson signed the measure on July 4, 1966, and it went into effect one year later. Johnson said at the time (it was also about a year before work started on the massive Pentagon Papers, which detailed incidents of official deception during the Johnson administration): "A democracy works best when the people have all the information that the security of the nation permits. No one should be able to pull curtains of secrecy around decisions which can be revealed without injury to the public interest."

The act set forth nine categories which the government could legally use to withhold information: By executive order "in the interest of the national defense or foreign policy"; in matters having to do only with "internal personnel rules and practices of an agency"; information "specifically exempted from disclosure by statute"; trade secrets and the like; certain inter- and intra-agency memos; personnel, medical, and similar files "the disclosure of which would constitute a clearly unwarranted invasion of personal privacy"; "investigatory files compiled for law enforcement purposes except to the extent available by law to a party other than an agency"; records of an agency which regulates financial institutions; and, geological and geophysical information concerning wells.

The consensus is that the law hasn't changed things much for the press. Some agencies frustrate questioners with the structure of the law itself (as in requiring them to specifically identify the document in question, or in charging as much as $3 to merely search for a piece of paper). One study of the implementation of the act, done for the Administrative Conference of the United States (a government agency), is itself "classified." The study bears the legend, "This report is not for publication or quotation. . . ." It concludes, among other things, that the press has not utilized the act very much, and that the law serves primarily those with "sufficient knowledge, interest and resources" to take advantage of it.

Congressman John E. Moss, who has fought for years for freedom of the press, would agree. In a speech in June, 1971, he said, "I must confess some disappointment that it has not been utilized as much as it should have. Unfortunately, despite its presence on the books, some people are still willing to accept a brush-off. . . . This includes the news media as well, who sometimes seem disinclined to spend the money and time to win their point by going to court."

Dr. Paul L. Fisher, Jr., the director of the Freedom of Information Center at the University of Missouri, made this comment on press freedom in general in an interview:

"It seems with every administration, we predict the imminent death of freedom of the press if things continue the way they're going. But I find it difficult to believe in this conspiracy theory—this idea that Nixon had it in for the press and that now he's sending Agnew and Mitchell out to settle the score. I just think it's been a very unhappy period in our national life, in which everybody's uptight. The president's uptight, the press is uptight, we're all uptight.

"We are just not as free a country as we were several years ago. The climate's different, and people are more careful of what they say. We're accepting more controls over our lives. We've gotten to the point where we *expect* more controls. We treat presidents as if they were kings."

JACK NELSON AND THE FBI

Jack Nelson, an investigative reporter for *The Los Angeles Times,* has come to this conclusion about the Federal Bureau of Investigation: "For so long they've been so sacrosanct that they just don't answer your questions if they don't want to." Here is why:

Late in December, 1970, Nelson and *Times* staffer Ronald J. Ostrow met with Thomas Bishop, assistant director of the FBI, to ask some questions about the agency. Bishop declined to answer; he asked that the reporters resubmit their questions in writing. On January 5, 1971, they sent in the questions, which had to do with the FBI's involvement with the television show, "The FBI"; reports of agents' being transferred to unpopular stations because they had said things J. Edgar Hoover didn't like, and so forth.

Bishop answered some of the questions in considerable detail. On January 12, Nelson and Ostrow sent another letter with 16 additional questions. They included such items as "What is the annual cost of carpeting Mr. Hoover's office . . . ?" and "Is there a standing order that Mr. Hoover's car should never leave on an out-of-town trip with him without having a new set of tires? We are told that such an order resulted because his car once suffered a flat between Washington and Valley Forge where he went to accept an award from the Freedoms Foundation. Is that true?" And "Did the FBI lab construct a big mahogany 'pirate's chest' with brass hinges and latches and put a case of Jack Daniel's Black Label in the chest and give it to him as a Christmas present some years ago?"

On January 14, Bishop replied: "The FBI is much too busy an organization to engage in the apparently endless exchange of question-and-answer correspondence which you obviously have in mind. Furthermore, your demands upon us have strong overtones of harassment, and some of the questions you have posed are so tainted with false and malicious implications that they frankly do not deserve the dignity of an acknowledgement."

Later, the writer of this report sent a letter to Bishop asking the assistant director why he had refused to answer the questions. He also was asked if he had ever referred to Nelson's drinking habits, and he was asked for comment on the reporter's charge that the FBI considered itself sacrosanct.

Bishop did not reply, but Hoover did. He wrote: "I am familiar with the exchange of correspondence between Mr. Bishop and Messrs. Nelson and Ostrow of the Los Angeles Times. I am thoroughly in agreement with Mr. Bishop's handling of this matter. Over the years it has been the policy of this Bureau to answer valid inquiries from the news media and the public. Mr. Bishop made every effort to cooperate in answering the inquiries of Messrs. Nelson and Ostrow until it became obvious that some of their questions were so tainted with false implications as to have strong overtones of harassment."

The Underground Press

Harassment by police against underground newspapers takes many forms, as was shown in a recent suit by the Washington Free Community against Jerry V. Wilson, the District of Columbia police chief, seeking to enjoin the police from further attacks on the press. Much of the harassment is directed against the young people who sell the newspapers on the street. In the Washington case, eight vendors of *The Washington Free Press* and *The Quicksilver Times* who appeared as witnesses counted about 300 episodes of harassment, including, said the suit: ". . . telling a vendor he needs a license to sell when he does not, ordering a vendor to move on when he's doing nothing wrong, kicking a vendor's newspapers into the streets, making a vendor take back a sale because he has put one foot into the street to hand a paper into an adjacent car, telling a vendor he cannot sell within sight of the White House, telling a vendor he cannot sell on a particular side of Connecticut Avenue, falsely claiming that store proprietors have registered a complaint about a vendor selling on the sidewalk in front of the store, offensive and heated verbal threats to 'get the fuck out of here because it is just you and me and I do not need any valid reason to arrest you,' and in at least one instance, the most outrageous kind of police misconduct in which a vendor is punched in the face, knocked to the ground, stepped on, manhandled to the police station, and then charged with 'Disorderly Conduct: To Wit, Lying on the Sidewalk'!"

Sometimes, as in the case of underground papers in New Orleans, the police first harass vendors and then attempt to suppress the paper at its source on the grounds that it is obscene, clearly in defiance of the Supreme Court test of obscenity. *The Washington Free Press* got into additional

50

trouble in northern Virginia on obscenity charges; at issue was a comic strip by R. Crum. At the time Virginia police were seizing the paper, the same and other Crum cartoons were on display, and for sale to the public, at Washington's DuPont Circle Corcoran Gallery of Art.

Other harassment is directed against young people who don't look straight when they appear with notebooks and cameras at news events, especially when they look closely at the police. Paul Cowan, writing in the *Village Voice* (June 10, 1971), told of a "period of intense harassment" undergone by two Roman Catholic nuns, associated with the left, at the hands of FBI agents. When Cowan attempted to take a picture of the agents' surveillance techniques, he said, one of them told him: "I'm giving you a forewarning. Don't shoot another picture of us or I'll break your camera."

Nat Hentoff has written of the tribulations of the Pacific Street Film Collective (in the *Village Voice,* starting June 3, 1971). The collective was making a film on surveillance techniques; after they made exterior location shots of the New York headquarters of the FBI and of the city police's Bureau of Special Services from an automobile registered in the name of a member's mother, she was visited by the police. A member was arrested for "filming without a permit," which he did not need; members were followed; agents interviewed the collective's neighbors and landlord; parents of members were told it was illegal to photograph FBI agents (it is not).

More recently there has been a small victory for the underground press. The Standing Committee of Correspondents of the U.S. Congress, five newsmen who make the rules for coverage at the Capitol, voted 3 to 2 to approve the accreditation of Tom Forcade, the Washington correspondent of the Underground Press Syndicate.

Forcade, who is perhaps best known for an appearance he made in 1970 at a hearing of the U.S. Commission on Obscenity and Pornography, at which he threw a cottage cheese pie into the face of a commission member, said in a recent interview that he planned to take his accreditation seriously, if he gets it. (The Rules Committees of Congress may overrule the Standing Committee's decision.) "I figure the worst thing I can do to them is report what's happening and how the others report it," he said.

THE CAMPUS PRESS

The many troubles of the campus press, like those of the underground press, are largely ignored by the "regular" channels of communication in America. And so they continue. Carl Nelson, the Washington editor of College Press Service, estimated recently that around 60 college and university newspapers were censored in one way or another during the 1970-71 academic year.

Censorship on the campus comes in many forms: Trustees, college administrators, student governments, legislatures, publication boards and faculty "advisors," printers who refuse to print material that angers them—and, undeniably, self-censorship, the worst kind. Student government itself seems to be a training ground for young politicians learning how to mistreat the press in later life. Mary Moudry, in the fall, 1969, issue of *College Press Review,* declared that "Allowing the student government to control the student portion of membership of a board of publications can lead to more censorship than most administrators would dream of."

Some examples from the 1970-71 academic year of campus press troubles, as collected by the College Press Service:

Student newspapers at branches of the University of California were subjected to regents' guidelines concerning "socio-political advocacy and the use of lewd and obscene articles and photographs" which made a mockery of the First Amendment.

In Denver, narcotics agents raided the offices of *The Paper,* at Metropolitan State College, and found nothing. Chuck Scott of the newspaper's staff wrote that thrice previously "narcotics or narcotics instruments have been planted in the office and found by staff members."

The Federal Communications Commission started investigating campus broadcast stations which operate on carrier current (not through radio waves). The commission asked questions such as "Does your system carry editorials or programs relating to controversial issues of public importance?"

The Internal Revenue Service investigated the tax exempt status of the Columbia University *Daily Spectator;* its stands on political candidates was a factor.

In Palo Alto, California, police raided the offices of the *Stanford Daily,* looking for photographs taken during a demonstration. In Lowell, Massachusetts, a disc jockey at the FM station run by Lowell Technological Institute was suspended from his job by a faculty advisor. The school felt the student had run afoul of the FCC's drug lyrics order by playing a song, "Hand of Doom," which is about the decline and approaching death of a heroin addict.

The staff of the *Reflector,* at Mississippi State University, which previously had been in trouble over an editorial stand on the death of God and another on whether evolution should be taught in the state, found that the locks had been changed on office doors after the word "shit" appeared in the paper.

· The staff of the *Concordian* at Concordia College was locked out because the newspaper ran advertisements about abortion referral and counseling. Numerous other campus papers have gotten into similar troubles.

The *Yellow Jacket,* at Waynesburg College in Pennsylvania, faced a rebellion by its printer when the phrase "fuck-up" was scheduled to appear in a news story.

And, according to College Press Service, "At Slippery Rock State College in Slippery Rock, Pennsylvania, the *Rocket* has had its funds frozen by the college administration because the paper has been printing news of events beyond the confines of the small western Pennsylvania campus. The school's administration, objecting particularly to the *Rocket's* use of (College Press Service) copy, is urging that the paper become an 'educational tool' to teach students 'the mechanics of journalism'."

POLICEMEN POSING AS NEWSMEN

Such are the tactics of surveillance organizations in this nation today that it is entirely possible for a nonviolent demonstration to be turned into a violent one by a participant who is actually on the payroll of a police agency, and for the demonstration to be covered by newsmen or people who appear to be newsmen, some of whom are on the payrolls of *other* police agencies. (For an examination of police surveillance activities, including the technique of posing as reporters, see Frank Donner's report, "The Theory and Practice of American Political Intelligence," in *The New York Review of Books*, April 22, 1971.)

Bona fide reporters make jokes about the police who frequently turn up at radicals' (and liberals') press conferences and demonstrations: FBI agents frequently are easy to spot because they seem unable to resist wearing hats, and it is said that Secret Service men frequently are observed talking into small paper bags with tiny aerials projecting out the top. But the presence of police in such situations has a chilling effect on everyone involved.

Paul Valentine, a reporter for *The Washington Post*, has covered many street confrontations and demonstrations. He was arrested in the police sweep of Resurrection City because "I was watching the police too closely." He said some dissident groups had been chilled to the extent that when they call press conferences, they require reporters to sign a register. As for himself, he said, "I have not felt intimidated yet. I'm aware that my picture has been taken several times. At some demonstrations—particularly those that I believe beforehand are going to be violent—I've worn rough clothes and I'm *sure* my picture's been taken then.

"But I don't think I'm intimidated by it. Offended and digusted by it, yes; but not intimidated. There's a desire to harass and ridicule the cops who're posing as newsmen. But I suppress it, because as a newsman, you're not supposed to do things like that—and also, the cop might arrest me for 'interfering with a policeman', even though he wouldn't identify himself as one."

13-100

ST. JOHN FISHER COLLEGE LIBRARY
PN4738 .P6
Powledge, Fred. cn   010101 000
The engineering of restraint;

0 1219 0030203 9